We All Fall Down

Riley Stratton

Presentation by *BookLeaf Publishing*

Web: www.bookleafpub.com

E-mail: info@bookleafpub.com

ISBN: 9789357616522

First edition 2022

*I have these amazing humans in my life
that are unbelievably great.*

*And there are some I've let down. And they
love me anyways, continue to support me,
endlessly. I know it's not easy, guys. Thank
you.*

*I will become a shining example of why you
don't give up on the people you love.*

I will be present

and I will be alive

and we will be happy.

Also, my badass dogs Nico and Kai.

ACKNOWLEDGEMENT

I am absolutely not a writer- just a woman with a some childish whims, dark humor, anxiety, pessimism, a bad attitude and a slight alcohol addiction.

PREFACE

At the beginning of this process, I was 10 days sober.

This has helped me keep busy, express my struggles and triumphs, and overall clear the fuckery out of my mind.

At the end of this process, I am 34 days sober.

Fuck yeah.

Begin

I am smiling
The floor is a cloud
I am smiling
The air is sweet
I am smiling
The euphoria is infinite
I am smiling
The sky is boundless
I am smiling
The sounds are echoes
Smiling
Close
Smiling
Closer
Smiling
Real

The smile breaks
The sound is real

I am confused
The ground is shaking
I am confused
The air is metal
I am confused

The hole is forming
I am confused
The world has opened
I am confused
The sounds are echoes
Confused
How
Confused
Why
Confused
Real

The smile breaks
The sound is real

I am awake
The tile is cold
I am awake
The air is rotten
I am awake
The pain is growing
I am awake
The reality knots inside
I am awake
The sounds are echoes
Awake
Reckless
Awake
Ashamed

Awake
Real

The smile breaks
The sound is real

I am in water
The air is pain
I am in water
The air is pain
I am in water
The air is pain
I am in water
The air is pain
I am in water
The sounds are echoes
Water
Pain
Water
Pain
Water
Real

The smile breaks
The sound is real

I am broken
The floor is on fire
I am broken

The walls are closing
I am broken
The room is dark
I am broken
The sounds are echoes
Broken
Defeated
Broken
Hollow
Broken
Real

The smile breaks
The sound is real

Intention

Remarkable
the lies we tell to be okay
The lies we create to feel
The doubt we push further down
As the truth loses appeal

Undoubtedly
the truth becomes distant sound
Not loud enough to hear
Slowly normality slips away
And they watch as we disappear

Losing
all memory of what was good
We are slipping into roles
Seeking to placate restless thought
Without surrendering our souls

The mind
becomes a dangerous place
Where all the dark thoughts dwell
The heart turns itself upside down
Our safe space ruined by the spell

Happiness

doesn't play here much
When it does, it isn't safe
Nothing here starts or ends
A clock stuck in place

Complacency
surrounds it all
Never striving to upgrade
Over and over - day to day
Our minds darkened by its shade

Loss
occurs only in the deepest lows
Like living in a cave
We succumb to it with soured grief
There's little left to save

The mind
is our greatest enemy
And the only end in sight
It screams to see the bitter end
We beg to see the light

Intent
is lost in every stage
The good - smaller and less
We beg to find a shred of hope
The solution is a guess

Help
exists in distant space
Not in reach of those in need
Dark floods all spaces of it
The bitter the hate the greed

Light
tries to come, tries
The spiral weave in our mind begins
Light, dark, light, dark, light
The real fight begins

BARRIERS

Bold blurs burn bright black
Allows Red Rage Into End
Radiating Shut

The Understanding

Hungry ghost
　hollow fire
　　deep tragic desire

Shining promises
　torn apart
　　neverending failing start

Abducted mind
　nagging repetition
　　endless internal competition

Sad eyes
　imitation smile
　　external concrete denial

Functioning peace
　believing normality
　　delayed internal calamity

Forced clarity
　suspended memories
　　marching mindless enemies

Sudden death

ruthlessly managed
    incapacitated afraid damaged

Placated pain
    enmeshed complications
        self inflicted violations

Explored remains
    darkened pathways
        uncovered finite always

Hopeful risk
    uncompromising crusade
        beautifully broken self-made

Held together
    smothering glue
        uplifted powerful true

Unstoppable change
    internal alignment
        inevitable inherent assignment

Brave unmasking
    bold intention
        silent happy comprehension

Departed

Eyes shut
Held breath
Frightened mind
Thick air

The longest moment

Instant memories
Vivd pictures
Jumbled sequence
Whirlwind colors
Frozen midair
Broken clock
Emotions afire
Fruitless efforts
Heart unmended
Final breath
Silent screams
Violent fear
Images slowing
Beautiful, alive
Red freckles
Brilliant blue
Lively smile
Alive.

Eyes open
Shakey exhale
Hands clench
You're gone.

Courage

In liquid strong
errant thoughts belong
putting broken minds at ease
a faux slice of peace
for as long as it lasts
numbing mistakes from the past
keeping bad thoughts at bay
to remember the following day
reasons are never hard to find
the solution always on the mind
never forgotten or unexcused
a mechanism that is abused
never offering permanent reprieve
hard evidence worn on the sleeves
a poor armor that doesn't hide
the awful messy things that are inside
another shot, a hit, a beer
anything to erase the fear
all consuming- all day, all night
no guarantees to win the fight
against melancholy, fucked up existence
positivity crushed with nagging persistence
what once was, is now a shell
walking dead in living hell
pleading for a hopeful light

wishing with tenacious fight
through the dark, a tiny glimmer
a light, a gleam, a hopeful shimmer
from deep in the chasm- it's bright!
beautiful, brilliant, breathtaking sight
a memory soars from deep in the heart
giving strength to break apart-
the walls, this prison that has built
can be shattered- the pain, the guilt
then, like lightning
vibrant, illuminating, frightening-

A chance

Dark

The tunnel is dark
Black like a cave
Run for your life
The danger is grave

The air feels stagnant
Harsh like thick smoke
Keep your feet moving
Don't let yourself choke

The path is so narrow
May not make it out
Running for your life
Your soul filled with doubt

Your tongue is tied
You cannot scream
You keep your feet moving
Is this a bad dream?

The madness is jolting
The walls reach like arms
You start running faster
Their intent is to harm

It feels like a circle
The odds feel so bleak
Keep your feet moving
Your spirit runs weak

The dark gets even darker
There's no up or down
Running for your life
In darkness you may drown

The path shows no weakness
You can feel it now, you know
Running for your life-

But perhaps it's time to slow

The still feels quite peaceful
Tired, you succumb
Your feet have ceased moving
The fear begins to numb

To turn yourself over
To finally end the fight
You have to stop running
And create an inner light

Inside you is the power
Brave and infinitely strong

Your feet keep you grounded
It was in you all along

The tunnel was a detour
A topsy-turvy distortion
You fought for your life
And overcome this misfortune

No road is final
You choose the way
You make the path
You have the say

Work in progress

Before is cemented
The past is concrete
We cannot make changes
Or rescind our deceit

To choose to do better
So simple to say
A little bit harder
To commit to everyday

Past actions don't define us
They exist in frozen time
Sometimes we think about them
Can't get them off our minds

This doesn't help our healing
Only continues to cause pain
Dwelling on the past
We make ourselves insane

We have all made poor choices
That is absolute fact
These are life's little lessons
To teach us how to act

We are a work in progress
A beautiful one, at that
So don't focus on the bad
Good will meet you where you're at

Be bold and assertive
Stand tall and shine bright
You owe the world nothing
This time you'll get it right

Panic!

Bellowing quiet
No sound in the air
The signs are so subtle
Yet alarmingly there

Just like a whisper
So soft and serene
The idea this time is different
Is distant and obscene

It comes with a smile
And then, with a frown
The feelings are tangled
And hard to breakdown

Emotions are twisted
No sorting them out
The panic is rising
Immense terrible doubt

Without outside forces
Or direction or idea
The panic changes motives
And this one is fear

Heart pounding drumbeats
Breaths shallow and strained
The next wave is cresting
Deep guilt and deep shame

And then, it's the movies
So clear and so true
The pictures scream loudly
With condescending hues

Drawn into it deeply
Tumbling down, farther away
The breath is now heavy heavy
Unable to stop, unable to steady

It's stays like this forever
Is simply how it seems
The transition so jolting
Confusion sewn in seams

Then the fog is lifted
As simply as it starts
The presence of this madness
Makes sanity fall apart

115

Rising from the ashes
Searching deep within
Soul-seeking, olive-branching
Big contagious grin

Coming from the trenches
Standing little chance
Now stopping to smell roses
And taking time to dance

Growth has become you
From deep within a soul
That was so deeply broken
And now is strong and whole

Overcoming every challenge
Reaching for the light
The battles never easy
Yet gracefully you fight

Speaking for the helpless
While making dreams come true
And never losing hope and sight
Of what makes you, you.

So many different choices
Times you wanted to stop
You continued on your pathway
You made it to the top

An entire life you've altered
Huge barriers you've slain
Inspiring those around you
To strive to do the same

You embraced the world so bravely
A wise friend you've become
To see what you've accomplished
The battles you have won

The world is your playground
The future is so bright
Let peace and health embrace you
And live life with all your might

Growth

Problem drinking
Never stopping; never thinking

Hitting low
Lacking pride; eating crow

Confronting doubt
Regret, pain; anxious throughout

Asking questions
Valued stories; learning lessons

Seeking improvement
Desired change; positive movement

Changing ways
Finding happiness; enjoying days

Inner healing
Coming back; entirely feeling

Mindful living
Being present; self-forgiving

Forward moving

Being positive; always improving

Honoring friends
Being honest; making amends

Continued desire
Inner peace; inner fire

Altered endings
Finding solace; finally mending

Being free
Becoming whole; beautifully me

Fire

Black eyes
Secretly hollow
Knowing, ominous
Flat, emotionless
Spinning spirals
Falling downward
Actively blinded
Seeking castles
Running empty
Losing balance
Played charades
Waning conscience
Bled dry
Smoking gun
Locked trauma
Covered footsteps
Bonded pain
Fixed choice
Cycled repeats
Plagued intention
Crowded space
Sickened mind
Wildly desperate
Awaiting death

Survivors

27

When stripped of a choice,
and not given a voice,
survive.

Madness

Melancholy music mumbles in monotone to melodies that monopolize the memories of malicious motives to manipulate.

Maddening

Mt. Recovery

The sharp jagged edges
Are lined by steep ledges
Narrow darkened pathways
Only travel halfway
Into the darkened sky
Where daylight doesn't try
The entire route obscene
Precarious and unclean
Littered with negative thoughts
And failed attempts once sought
Billowing wind whips through
With a familiar gloomy hue
Encompassing all empty space
Memories echoes from a distant place
Up high, shapes begin to appear
Present, bold, yet unclear
The message is not evident
Confusion and discontent
Pushing forward feels right
Requiring courageous might
The steps are hard; and slow; and fast
Each one harder than the last
Nothing seems to make a change
Objects move and rearrange
The mountain continues growing more

Spinning around an invisible core
The heart of all nestled inside
Within the problem, the solution resides
Suddenly the air is warm
Lucid thoughts begin to form
Realizing there is a way
Negativity and doubt begin to sway
Seeking only the easy solution
Left behind chaos and confusion
Reaching deep to create the shift
Fear and doubt begin to lift
Feeling resilient and tough, pushing past
breaking barriers, until the last
Looking back, it's understood
The path was scary, dangerous but good
The steps were taken- so brave and strong
Recovery was at the top all along.

One World

Night is here, daylight has past
The light above can never last
Phases here, they ebb and flow
A constant morphing spiritual show
Within this show, many plots arise
Tales of wonder and surprise
Lives lived fully genuine and true
Some blissfully older, some brand new
There's laughter here, hearty sounds
There is no limit and no bounds
Alongside this delightful place
Are some who live in a darker space
Lives of gloom and hate and fear
Niceties are rare to hear
Unlucky folk with big issues
Who lie and steal, hurt and abuse
Existing in one universe
Individuals so diverse
To be at peace, we must find
A way to leave judgment behind
To embrace deeply with light and hope
And allow our minds a larger scope
A mind of kindness and selfless intent
Living within means, being content
Simply put: we have a chance

To do this right, to change our stance
To get along, and be kind
Never leaving anyone behind
Take care of yourself and each other
Value and honor one another
Be mindful and learn to be free,
Avoid endless conflict and learn to just be.

The Bottom

My stomach is hollow
My head will follow

Counting each and every second
Invisible hands with which I'm beckoned

An aching void deep within
A constant battle I will not win

Failing each attempt to stop
Deeper and lower my self-esteem drops

Tried to cut back, tried to pace
Hard to look at my own face

Every night the race is on
Up all night until the dawn

Making myself tired and ill
A mental hold that has me still

Unable to make coherent choices
Not comprehending familiar voices

Forgetting what I said before

Puking on the bathroom floor

Disappointed looks but I don't care
I am only vaguely aware

Of what I've done and what I'm doing
Through tunneled mind is what I'm viewing

"One more time, I think I can!"
Never goes according to plan

To realize the absolute weight
I had to fuck up and try to tempt fate

A violent bottom I had hit
Dug myself into a pit

The aftermath sparked several things
Consequences which mistakes bring

Guilt and fear and hate and shame
Pain and unshakeable feelings of blame

That bottom is lower than low
My anxious mind is beginning to slow

"What's meant to be, will be" they say
My pessimism begins to sway

It can get better- it can and has
By living in the present, not the future or past

I love you more

May you be all you ever dreamed
Find peace from within

May your light never lose it's gleam
And you keep your bright, contagious grin

May the world not harden you
And you always have a choice

May your intentions always be true
And you always have a voice

May you not make mistakes as I
Or feel deliberate pain

May you recognize the beauty of the sky
And find a rainbow in the rain

May you be what you want to become
And experience all the best

May you have a life you're not running from
Existence is not a test

May you be happy as can be

And always feel acceptance

May you please always allow me to see
Your extraordinary transcendence